ALTO SAX

2ND EDITION

THE BEST OF
The Beatles

ISBN 978-0-7935-2144-9

HAL•LEONARD®
CORPORATION
7777 W. BLUEMOUND RD. P.O. BOX 13819 MILWAUKEE, WI 53213

Visit Hal Leonard Online at
www.halleonard.com

CONTENTS

ALL MY LOVING

ALTO SAX

Words and Music by JOHN LENNON
and PAUL McCARTNEY

ACROSS THE UNIVERSE

ALTO SAX

Words and Music by JOHN LENNON
and PAUL McCARTNEY

ALL YOU NEED IS LOVE

ALTO SAX

Words and Music by JOHN LENNON
and PAUL McCARTNEY

AND I LOVE HER

ALTO SAX

Words and Music by JOHN LENNON
and PAUL McCARTNEY

BACK IN THE U.S.S.R.

ALTO SAX

Words and Music by JOHN LENNON
and PAUL McCARTNEY

THE BALLAD OF JOHN AND YOKO

ALTO SAX

Words and Music by JOHN LENNON
and PAUL McCARTNEY

BECAUSE

ALTO SAX

Words and Music by JOHN LENNON
and PAUL McCARTNEY

BIRTHDAY

ALTO SAX

Words and Music by JOHN LENNON
and PAUL McCARTNEY

Moderately fast Rock

BLACKBIRD

ALTO SAX

Words and Music by JOHN LENNON
and PAUL McCARTNEY

CAN'T BUY ME LOVE

ALTO SAX

Words and Music by JOHN LENNON
and PAUL McCARTNEY

COME TOGETHER

ALTO SAX

Words and Music by JOHN LENNON
and PAUL McCARTNEY

A DAY IN THE LIFE

ALTO SAX

Words and Music by JOHN LENNON
and PAUL McCARTNEY

DAY TRIPPER

ALTO SAX

Words and Music by JOHN LENNON
and PAUL McCARTNEY

DEAR PRUDENCE

ALTO SAX

Words and Music by JOHN LENNON
and PAUL McCARTNEY

DO YOU WANT TO KNOW A SECRET?

ALTO SAX

Words and Music by JOHN LENNON
and PAUL McCARTNEY

DRIVE MY CAR

ALTO SAX

Words and Music by JOHN LENNON
and PAUL McCARTNEY

EIGHT DAYS A WEEK

ALTO SAX

Words and Music by JOHN LENNON
and PAUL McCARTNEY

ELEANOR RIGBY

ALTO SAX

Words and Music by JOHN LENNON
and PAUL McCARTNEY

EVERY LITTLE THING

ALTO SAX

Words and Music by JOHN LENNON
and PAUL McCARTNEY

THE FOOL ON THE HILL

ALTO SAX

Words and Music by JOHN LENNON
and PAUL McCARTNEY

FROM ME TO YOU

ALTO SAX

Words and Music by JOHN LENNON
and PAUL McCARTNEY

GET BACK

ALTO SAX

Words and Music by JOHN LENNON
and PAUL McCARTNEY

GIRL

ALTO SAX

Words and Music by JOHN LENNON
and PAUL McCARTNEY

GOLDEN SLUMBERS

ALTO SAX

Words and Music by JOHN LENNON
and PAUL McCARTNEY

GOOD DAY SUNSHINE

ALTO SAX

Words and Music by JOHN LENNON
and PAUL McCARTNEY

GOT TO GET YOU INTO MY LIFE

ALTO SAX

Words and Music by JOHN LENNON
and PAUL McCARTNEY

A HARD DAY'S NIGHT

ALTO SAX

Words and Music by JOHN LENNON
and PAUL McCARTNEY

HELLO, GOODBYE

ALTO SAX

Words and Music by JOHN LENNON
and PAUL McCARTNEY

HELP!

ALTO SAX

Words and Music by JOHN LENNON
and PAUL McCARTNEY

HELTER SKELTER

ALTO SAX

Words and Music by JOHN LENNON
and PAUL McCARTNEY

HERE COMES THE SUN

ALTO SAX

Words and Music by
GEORGE HARRISON

HERE, THERE AND EVERYWHERE

ALTO SAX

Words and Music by JOHN LENNON
and PAUL McCARTNEY

HEY JUDE

ALTO SAX

Words and Music by JOHN LENNON
and PAUL McCARTNEY

I FEEL FINE

ALTO SAX

Words and Music by JOHN LENNON
and PAUL McCARTNEY

I AM THE WALRUS

ALTO SAX

Words and Music by JOHN LENNON
and PAUL McCARTNEY

I SAW HER STANDING THERE

ALTO SAX

Words and Music by JOHN LENNON
and PAUL McCARTNEY

Moderately bright, with a beat

I SHOULD HAVE KNOWN BETTER

ALTO SAX

Words and Music by JOHN LENNON
and PAUL McCARTNEY

I WANT TO HOLD YOUR HAND

ALTO SAX

Words and Music by JOHN LENNON
and PAUL McCARTNEY

I WILL

ALTO SAX

Words and Music by JOHN LENNON
and PAUL McCARTNEY

I'LL CRY INSTEAD

ALTO SAX

Words and Music by JOHN LENNON
and PAUL McCARTNEY

I'LL FOLLOW THE SUN

ALTO SAX

Words and Music by JOHN LENNON
and PAUL McCARTNEY

I'M A LOSER

ALTO SAX

Words and Music by JOHN LENNON
and PAUL McCARTNEY

Moderately

I'M HAPPY JUST TO DANCE WITH YOU

ALTO SAX

Words and Music by JOHN LENNON
and PAUL McCARTNEY

I'VE JUST SEEN A FACE

ALTO SAX

Words and Music by JOHN LENNON
and PAUL McCARTNEY

IF I FELL

ALTO SAX

Words and Music by JOHN LENNON
and PAUL McCARTNEY

IN MY LIFE

ALTO SAX

Words and Music by JOHN LENNON
and PAUL McCARTNEY

IT WON'T BE LONG

ALTO SAX

Words and Music by JOHN LENNON
and PAUL McCARTNEY

IT'S ONLY LOVE

ALTO SAX

Words and Music by JOHN LENNON
and PAUL McCARTNEY

JULIA

ALTO SAX

Words and Music by JOHN LENNON
and PAUL McCARTNEY

LADY MADONNA

ALTO SAX

Words and Music by JOHN LENNON
and PAUL McCARTNEY

LET IT BE

ALTO SAX

Words and Music by JOHN LENNON
and PAUL McCARTNEY

THE LONG AND WINDING ROAD

ALTO SAX

Words and Music by JOHN LENNON
and PAUL McCARTNEY

LOVE ME DO

ALTO SAX

Words and Music by JOHN LENNON
and PAUL McCARTNEY

LUCY IN THE SKY WITH DIAMONDS

ALTO SAX

Words and Music by JOHN LENNON
and PAUL McCARTNEY

MAGICAL MYSTERY TOUR

ALTO SAX

Words and Music by JOHN LENNON
and PAUL McCARTNEY

MARTHA MY DEAR

ALTO SAX

Words and Music by JOHN LENNON
and PAUL McCARTNEY

MICHELLE

ALTO SAX

Words and Music by JOHN LENNON
and PAUL McCARTNEY

NO REPLY

ALTO SAX

Words and Music by JOHN LENNON
and PAUL McCARTNEY

NORWEGIAN WOOD

(This Bird Has Flown)

ALTO SAX

Words and Music by JOHN LENNON
and PAUL McCARTNEY

NOWHERE MAN

ALTO SAX

Words and Music by JOHN LENNON
and PAUL McCARTNEY

OB-LA-DI, OB-LA-DA

ALTO SAX

Words and Music by JOHN LENNON
and PAUL McCARTNEY

OCTOPUS'S GARDEN

ALTO SAX

Words and Music by RICHARD STARKEY,
JOHN LENNON and PAUL McCARTNEY

PAPERBACK WRITER

ALTO SAX

Words and Music by JOHN LENNON
and PAUL McCARTNEY

Bright Rock

PENNY LANE

ALTO SAX

Words and Music by JOHN LENNON
and PAUL McCARTNEY

PLEASE PLEASE ME

ALTO SAX

Words and Music by JOHN LENNON
and PAUL McCARTNEY

P.S. I LOVE YOU

ALTO SAX

Words and Music by JOHN LENNON
and PAUL McCARTNEY

REVOLUTION

ALTO SAX

Words and Music by JOHN LENNON
and PAUL McCARTNEY

RUN FOR YOUR LIFE

ALTO SAX

Words and Music by JOHN LENNON
and PAUL McCARTNEY

SGT. PEPPER'S LONELY HEARTS CLUB BAND

ALTO SAX

Words and Music by JOHN LENNON
and PAUL McCARTNEY

SHE LOVES YOU

ALTO SAX

Words and Music by JOHN LENNON
and PAUL McCARTNEY

SHE'S A WOMAN

ALTO SAX

Words and Music by JOHN LENNON
and PAUL McCARTNEY

SOMETHING

ALTO SAX

Words and Music by
GEORGE HARRISON

STRAWBERRY FIELDS FOREVER

ALTO SAX

Words and Music by JOHN LENNON
and PAUL McCARTNEY

TELL ME WHY

ALTO SAX

Words and Music by JOHN LENNON
and PAUL McCARTNEY

THANK YOU GIRL

ALTO SAX

Words and Music by JOHN LENNON
and PAUL McCARTNEY

THINGS WE SAID TODAY

ALTO SAX

Words and Music by JOHN LENNON
and PAUL McCARTNEY

THIS BOY
(Ringo's Theme)

ALTO SAX

Words and Music by JOHN LENNON
and PAUL McCARTNEY

TICKET TO RIDE

ALTO SAX

Words and Music by JOHN LENNON
and PAUL McCARTNEY

Moderate Rock

TWIST AND SHOUT

ALTO SAX

Words and Music by BERT RUSSELL
and PHIL MEDLEY

WE CAN WORK IT OUT

ALTO SAX

Words and Music by JOHN LENNON
and PAUL McCARTNEY

WHEN I'M SIXTY-FOUR

ALTO SAX

Words and Music by JOHN LENNON
and PAUL McCARTNEY

WHILE MY GUITAR GENTLY WEEPS

ALTO SAX

Words and Music by
GEORGE HARRISON

WITH A LITTLE HELP FROM MY FRIENDS

ALTO SAX

Words and Music by JOHN LENNON
and PAUL McCARTNEY

THE WORD

ALTO SAX

Words and Music by JOHN LENNON
and PAUL McCARTNEY

YELLOW SUBMARINE

ALTO SAX

Words and Music by JOHN LENNON
and PAUL McCARTNEY

March tempo

YES IT IS

ALTO SAX

Words and Music by JOHN LENNON
and PAUL McCARTNEY

YESTERDAY

ALTO SAX

Words and Music by JOHN LENNON
and PAUL McCARTNEY

YOU CAN'T DO THAT

ALTO SAX

Words and Music by JOHN LENNON
and PAUL McCARTNEY

YOU WON'T SEE ME

ALTO SAX

Words and Music by JOHN LENNON
and PAUL McCARTNEY

YOU'RE GOING TO LOSE THAT GIRL

ALTO SAX

Words and Music by JOHN LENNON
and PAUL McCARTNEY

YOU'VE GOT TO HIDE YOUR LOVE AWAY

ALTO SAX

Words and Music by JOHN LENNON
and PAUL McCARTNEY

YOUR MOTHER SHOULD KNOW

ALTO SAX

Words and Music by JOHN LENNON
and PAUL McCARTNEY